THE SHREW WITH THE FLU!

WRITTEN BY
WILL HAMILTON-DAVIES

ILLUSTRATED BY
JENNIFER DAVISON

SilverWood

Published in 2020 by SilverWood Books

SilverWood Books Ltd
14 Small Street, Bristol, BS1 1DE, United Kingdom
www.silverwoodbooks.co.uk

Copyright © Will Hamilton-Davies 2020
Images © Jennifer Davison 2020

The right of Will Hamilton-Davies to be identified as the author of this work
has been asserted in accordance with the Copyright, Designs and
Patents Act 1988 Sections 77 and 78.

All rights reserved. No part of this publication may be reproduced,
stored in a retrieval system, or transmitted in any form or by any means,
electronic, mechanical, photocopying, recording or otherwise,
without prior permission of the copyright holder.

This is a work of fiction. Names, characters, places and incidents either are
products of the author's imagination or are used fictitiously. Any resemblance
to actual events or locales or persons, living or dead, is entirely coincidental.

ISBN 978-1-78132-982-5 (paperback)
ISBN 978-1-78132-983-2 (hardback)
ISBN 978-1-80042-016-8 (ebook)

British Library Cataloguing in Publication Data
A CIP catalogue record for this book is available from the British Library

Nestling under a leafy tree,
A greedy shrew could hardly see.
His eyes were small, his sight was bad,
But what a nose this small shrew had.

His long thin snout would smell the way
To find his food from day to day.
Across the forest floor he went,
Seeking out his food by scent.

But on one day, between the trees,
Where morning sun broke through the leaves,

Shrew had left his usual trail,
Tracking down a scrumptious snail.

Into rocks and trees he knocked.

He had bad sight, and now no smell,

And as he ran, he tripped and fell.

A branch had fallen from a tree.
"THIS WORM will have to BE MY TEA!"

The small shrew said and ate a stick,
Which left him feeling rather sick.
He gobbled up what was still there,
Then looked for extra food elsewhere.

"YUM!
A woodlouse,
MY FAVOURITE
LUNCH!"

Shrew wondered why there was no crunch.
Small Shrew had eaten nothing more
Than damp black dirt straight from the floor!

He thought he'd found a centipede.

"THIS IS EXACTLY what I NEED!"

He said and took a massive bite.
A little plain, but quite alright.
He'd always eaten like a king,

But now this shrew was EATING STRING!

SOME BEES or ANTS a STEAK, a nice LONG SNAKE

He was unsure of what to do,
Then, in an instant, small Shrew knew.

He didn't have to use his smell,
his ears could hear bugs just as well.

BUZZ BUZZ

The bees would always buzz around.

HISSSSS

A snake would make a hissing sound.

The crickets chirped.

CHIRP CHIRP

The birds would sing.

This shrew could HEAR EVERYTHING!

He munched on beetles, ants and flies
Of every shape and every size.
He filled his belly to the top,

But now this shrew

JUST COULD NOT STOP!

He'd eaten mud and twigs and string,
And now he would not spare a thing.

He munched on all the food he could,
And ate his way through half the wood...

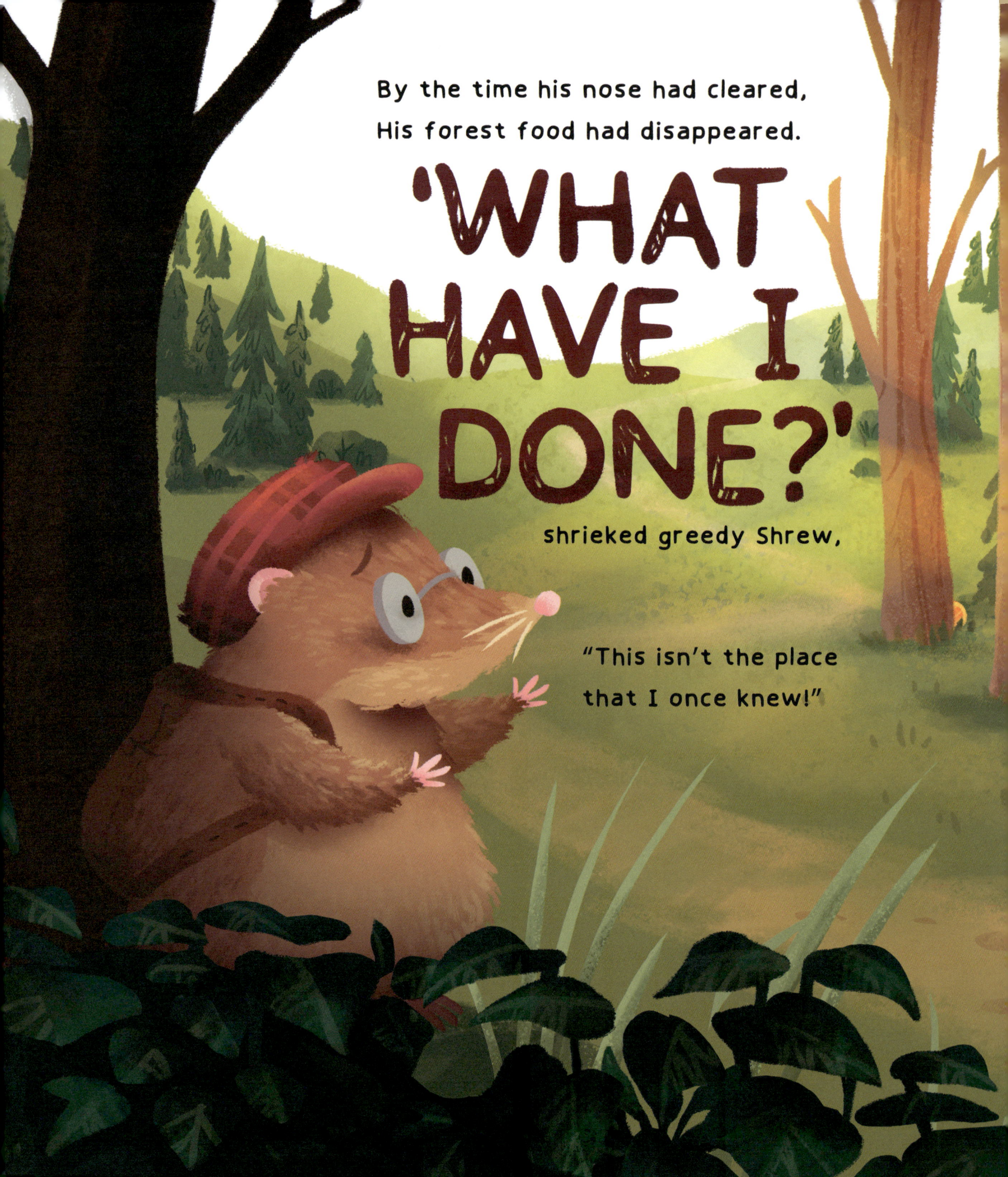

By the time his nose had cleared,
His forest food had disappeared.

'WHAT HAVE I DONE?' shrieked greedy Shrew,

"This isn't the place that I once knew!"

He couldn't smell delicious bugs,
Like bees and ants and worms and slugs.

He ate them all while he was ill,
And now his lively wood... was still.

Perched upon a mossy rock,
Shrew was sad; he sat in shock.

His nose was clear.
His eyes were wide.

He felt a sadness
deep inside.

This was not his happy home.
Without the bugs, he felt alone.

He knew he had TO DO SOME GOOD,

To try and save this lovely wood.

Shrew began to give and share,
And think about the

WORLD with CARE.

He scattered seeds and helped the bees

BY CARING for the PLANTS AND TREES.

Nature soon began its fight,
Bouncing back with all its might.
The bugs returned. The bushes grew.
Berries glistened red and blue.

And little Shrew forever knew,
The good that little deeds could do.

When hunting, he was twice as speedy,

But never again was this shrew GREEDY!

Acknowledgements

Thanks to everyone that supported this project through Kickstarter; I feel incredibly lucky to have you supporting me along this journey! Special mentions go to:

Heather Frankham

Aamir & Zain Charania

Benedict Thomas Lee

Max & Emily Hamilton-Davies

Evie Cloes

Eloise Ruth Auld

mrsbeesgarden

Ollie Vallance

The Kings

Of course, this book wouldn't exist in the form that it does if it weren't for the incredible work of Jennifer Davison (@jen_sketch) and the relentless support of Darren from Kabloom, as well as my family.

About the Author

As one of six, Will Hamilton-Davies spent most of his young adult life entertaining three much younger siblings — much of which involved reading stories. Though his ability as a writer was solidified some years before — while pursuing English at secondary school and Journalism at Newcastle University — it wasn't until his graduation year that Will discovered a relentless passion for rhyming picture books; in fact, it was around this time that retired primary school teacher, Sheila Supple, was the first to advise Will to pursue authorship, as his writing was "crying out for illustration". Will's stories are instilled with themes of morality and kindness, and he likes nothing more than to sit with a group of avid listeners and bring these wonderful worlds to life.

Instagram, Facebook, and Twitter @willhdofficial

kickstarter.com/profile/theshrewwiththeflu